Contents

Always Be Prepared!

Do you want to use your science skills to solve crimes? This is what forensic scientists do. They collect evidence from the scene of a crime, and then they do tests to try to discover when it was committed and how—and who might have done it.

Think your crime-fighting skills are up to scratch? When you've solved the puzzles in this book, they will be!

The criminal may have left traces at the crime scene—this is called "trace evidence"!

Knowledge of the human body might give us clues about the criminal.

Tests can reveal if the criminal used itching powder, explosives, or even poison!

Broken glass, splatters, and car tracks reveal how the crime was commited.

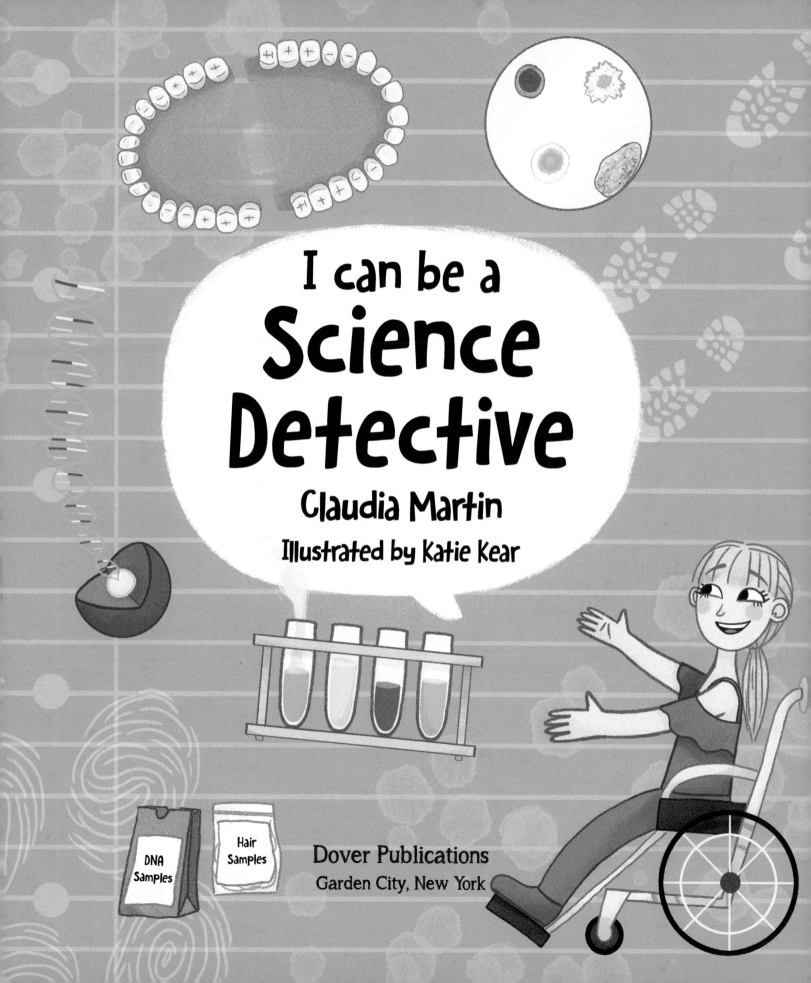

I can be a
Science
Detective

Claudia Martin

Illustrated by Katie Kear

Dover Publications
Garden City, New York

DNA Samples

Hair Samples

Bibliographical Note

This Dover edition, first published in 2019, is an unabridged
republication of the work published by Arcturus Publishing Limited,
London, in 2019.

International Standard Book Number

ISBN-13: 978-0-486-83921-9
ISBN-10: 0-486-83921-4

Manufactured in the United States by LSC Communications Book LLC
83921403
www.doverpublications.com

4 6 8 10 9 7 5 3

2021

What is STEM?

STEM is a world-wide initiative that aims to cultivate an interest in Science, Technology, Engineering, and Mathematics, in an effort to promote these disciplines to as wide a variety of students as possible.

Project: Pack Your Bag!

Before you head to your first crime scene, pack your bag. As well as equipment for collecting evidence, you need to take a clean body suit, face mask, and gloves, so you don't leave traces of yourself at the scene.

Equipment for Collecting Evidence:

- Camera
- Chemicals for tests
- Crime scene suit
- Evidence bags and labels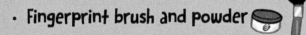
- Fingerprint brush and powder
- Gloves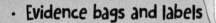

- Magnifying glass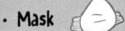
- Mask
- Notebook and pen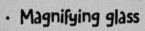
- Test tubes
- Tweezers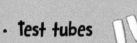

Which of these bags contains everything on the list?

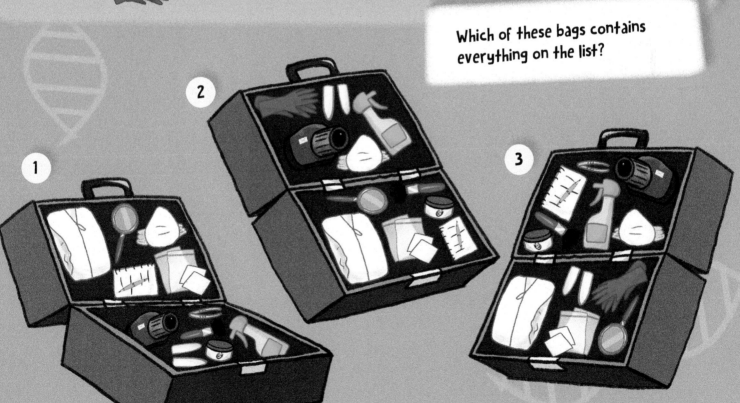

Find Fingerprints

The skin on your fingertips is covered in patterns of tiny ridges. When you touch shiny surfaces, your sweat leaves a mark in the shape of these fingertip patterns, called fingerprints. Forensic scientists can see these prints more clearly by dusting them with powder.

Each person has a slightly different set of patterns. If there are fingerprints at a crime scene, you might be able to identify who made them!

Although your fingerprints are unique, the same types of shapes show up in everyone's prints. They're called arches, loops, and whorls.

Arch

Loop

Double loop

Mixed figure

Whorl

Project: take Your Prints

When police officers arrest a suspect, they often make a record of their fingerprints using ink and paper. Try recording your own fingerprints! Can you see any arches, loops, or whorls?

You will need:

- two pieces of white paper
- A blunt pencil
- tape
- Scissors

1. Use a pencil to scribble on paper, going over the same area again and again.

2. Rub a clean, dry fingertip over the patch.

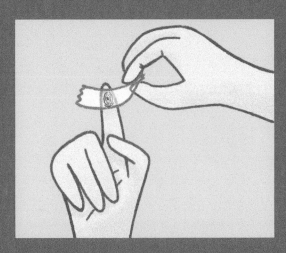

3. Stick a piece of tape over the fingertip, then pull gently away. Now you have a record of your print.

4. Stick the tape onto a clean piece of paper and label it. Repeat steps 1–4 with your other fingers —or with friends and family.

Examine Footprints

Sometimes footprints are left by a criminal at a crime scene, often pressed into mud. Scientists can record these prints by filling them with liquid plaster, which will harden into a solid. Then they can compare them to the shoes of suspects to place them at the scene.

Different types or brands of shoes have slightly different patterns on their soles.

Take a look at the soles of your shoes. The prints left by your shoes are almost as unique as your fingerprints.

Everyone walks differently, by scuffing their heels or pressing harder with the outsides of their feet.

Project: Who Ate the Cookies?

Someone has eaten all the freshly baked cookies at Fairmeadow Farm. Follow the footprints and use your crime-solving skills to find out which suspect ate them!

Suspect 1
Farmer Fiona

Suspect 2
Farmer Fred

Suspect 3
Sam the Sheepdog

Suspect 4
Percy the Pig

Suspect 5
Gertrude Goose

Suspect 6
Merlin Magpie

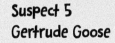

Collect DNA

Cells are the tiny building blocks that make up your body. Nearly every cell in your body contains long, thin molecules of DNA. DNA contains the instructions that tell your cells exactly how to grow and function. These are passed down from parents to their children. They tell your body to have, for example, red or black hair, and brown or blue eyes.

Since humans are pretty similar, 99.9% of your DNA is identical to everybody else's. But 0.1% of your DNA is unique to you. So, if you can find a sample of someone's DNA, you have an amazing record of that person.

DNA is the shape of a twisted ladder called a double helix.

There are thousands of rungs on each DNA ladder, giving a string of instructions.

There are around 37 trillion tiny cells in the human body.

DNA is bundled up in the nucleus of most cells.

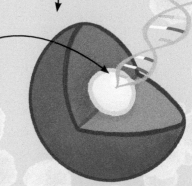

Project: Search for Samples!

Forensic scientists can find DNA in flakes of skin, nail clippings, and hair. They can also collect it from body fluids, such as blood, sweat, vomit, tears, earwax, pee, poop, saliva (dribble), and mucus (snot). Grab your evidence bags, and circle 5 items in this hotel room that might contain DNA samples.

... And Examine DNA

When forensic scientists have collected material containing DNA, they take it to a lab. First, they extract, or take out, the DNA from its cell. Then they study the DNA to see if it matches up with DNA taken from suspects.

Studying someone's DNA cannot tell us exactly how they look or behave, because human beings are very complex. But here are 5 things that DNA can tell us about an unknown suspect:

1. If they are likely to have light (e.g., blue, green), dark (brown and black), or hazel eyes.

2. If they are likely to have red hair.

3. If they are the same person as, or in the same family as, someone who has already given a DNA sample.

4. If they are male or female.

5. If they have a high risk of suffering from certain diseases that are passed through a family's DNA.

Project: Extract DNA From a Strawberry

Strawberry cells contain lots of DNA molecules—much more than human cells—so they are quite easy to extract and see. A single molecule of DNA is too thin to see with the naked eye, but this experiment makes the strands of strawberry DNA clump together, so we can take a look.

You will need:

! You will need an adult to pour and measure the rubbing alcohol!

- 1 tablespoon (14.7 ml) rubbing alcohol
- 6 tablespoons (88 ml) water
- 2 teaspoons (10 ml) dishwashing liquid
- ¼ teaspoon salt
- 1 strawberry
- Measuring container
- Measuring spoon
- Zip-seal freezer bag
- Strainer/sieve
- Bowl
- Tall drinking glass
- tweezers

1. Put the strawberry in a freezer bag, then pour in the water, dishwashing liquid, and salt. Remove as much air from the bag as possible, then seal it.

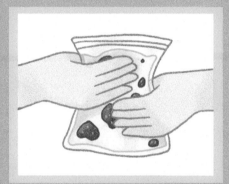

2. Press the bag with your fingers for at least 2 minutes to thoroughly mash up the strawberry. The soap and salt break down the fruit's cells so that they release their DNA.

3. Press the mash through a strainer into a bowl. Then pour it from the bowl into a tall glass.

4. Ask an adult to gently drip 1 tablespoon of chilled rubbing alcohol onto the surface of the strawberry liquid.

5. You will see a layer of white, stringy goop near the top of the mixture—this is strawberry DNA! Use tweezers to pull out the DNA, and take a good look at it!

Leaving a Trace

DNA is not the only trace that criminals can leave at a scene. Other types of "trace evidence" include powder from their makeup, the fluff from their sweater, or soil from their boots. If a driver has crashed into another car and sped away, there may be traces of paint from their own car.

Soil is a mixture of grains of rock, dead plants and animals, water, and air. The exact mixture differs from place to place. Identifying the soil on someone's boots might tell us where they have been.

Soil can be sandy, chalky, or sticky with clay.

Soil may contain seeds or pollen from plants that grow in only one area.

Soil may be mixed with animal droppings that can be identified.

Project: Track the Trace Evidence!

Someone has broken into the Modern Art Museum and stolen a priceless masterpiece! Examine the trace evidence found at the scene of the crime, then decide which suspect to call in for questioning.

Trace Evidence Found:

- A footprint with traces of mud and red paint
- A wisp of black yarn
- A long blond hair

The Suspects:

Suspect A is a gardener and janitor.

Suspect B is a nurse.

Suspect C is a landscape painter.

Contaminated Evidence

Trace evidence must be carefully collected, stored, and tested. If not, it could become contaminated, which is when it is spoiled by contact with another material. For example, a forensic scientist might contaminate a DNA sample with their own DNA by accidentally spitting on it—which is why masks are always worn!

If a forensic scientist makes a mistake, the wrong person could be arrested— even imprisoned—for a crime. Here are 4 tips to avoid contamination:

1. Limit the number of people who enter the crime scene until the evidence has been collected.

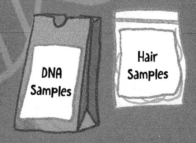

DNA Samples

Hair Samples

2. Everyone who visits the crime scene must wear a brand-new suit, mask, and gloves.

3. Bag and label evidence carefully.

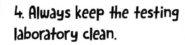
4. Always keep the testing laboratory clean.

Project: Spot the Differences!

This crime scene has been contaminated, so it is lucky that you took a photograph when you first arrived. Spot the 5 examples of contamination.

time: 10 a.m.

time: 4 p.m.

Dental Detectives

Everyone has a unique set of teeth. Teeth are different sizes and shapes. Your dentist has a record of your teeth, because he or she keeps the X-rays that were taken when checking for cavities. If someone lost their memory, it might be possible to identify them using their dental records.

Children have 20 teeth by about the age of 3. Adults have up to 32 teeth, the final "wisdom" teeth growing in at 17–21 years old. In adults, teeth wear down from a lifetime of chewing.

Canines, which are used for ripping food, are more pointed.

Incisors help you bite off food.

Molars, which are flatter, are for grinding up food.

"Wisdom" teeth are the final molars to emerge.

Project: Chocolate Bites!

Since everyone's teeth are slightly different, everyone leaves a different bite mark. When a thief broke into Cherry's Chocolate Shop, they made a silly mistake—they bit into a bar of chocolate and then left it behind, giving us a record of their bite. Which suspect bit the chocolate?

the Suspects:

Suspect 1

Suspect 2

Suspect 3

Suspect 4

How tall?

People with smaller feet and hands, and shorter legs and arms, usually are shorter overall. In fact, the human body usually obeys certain rules. This means that forensic scientists can make guesses about someone's height by measuring the size of their feet and the length of their steps in their footprints. They can even guess how tall a robber is by measuring how far they have reached in through an open car window.

Adults' bodies usually follow these rules more exactly than children's bodies, since kids grow in stops and starts. And some adults don't quite follow the rules either!

Arm span (inches or cm) = Height (inches or cm)

Step length (inches or cm) x 2.5 = Height (inches or cm)

Foot length (inches or cm) x 6.6 = Height (inches or cm)

Project: Reaching Out!

Test out the idea that arm span is roughly equal to height.

You will need:

- A tape measure
- Pencil and paper
- A measuring partner

1. Stand with your arms straight out to the sides.

2. Ask your partner to measure from the middle finger of your left hand to the middle finger of your right hand.

3. Record the measurement.

4. Take off your shoes, then stand against a wall with your feet together and your back straight.

5. Ask your partner to hold the tape measure level with the top of your head. While they hold it in place, read off the bottom of the tape.

6. Record the measurement from step 5, then swap with your partner to take their measurements.

Is your arm span equal to your height? If not, was it less than 2 inches (5 cm) bigger or smaller than your height? Was your partner's? Do you think you have proved that arm span is roughly equal to height?

Shadow Shapes

Eyewitnesses may make confused statements. Forensic scientists understand how light and darkness affect what we think we are seeing. For example, white and yellow cars look the same under streetlights, and a dark blue or brown coat can look black in dim light.

- Opaque objects cast dark shadows because light cannot pass through them.
- Transparent objects, like clear glass and water, let light pass through them, so they do not cast a shadow.
- Translucent objects, like stained glass, block some light, casting a faint shadow.

The lower the source of light, the longer the shadow.

As an object moves farther away from a light source, its shadow grows smaller.

Sometimes a witness has only glimpsed shadows, so it is useful to understand how shadows are made.

Was one of these robbers really much taller than the other?

Project: Glass Game!

The security guard at the Glass Museum was doodling in her sketchbook when a thief tiptoed away with a priceless vase. All the guard remembers is a strange shadow crossing her page. Luckily, she sketched the shadow. Which of these suspects could have cast the shadow?

Suspect 1

Suspect 2

Suspect 3

Suspect 4

Making a Noise

Sometimes witnesses to a crime hear something—a car speeding off or glass shattering. Sounds are made when an object vibrates, shaking from side to side. This makes the surrounding air vibrate, and the vibrations travel outward as "sound waves." When the waves reach your eardrum, they make it vibrate—and you hear sounds.

Quiet sounds like whispers do not travel far, as the sound waves get smaller and soon disappear. Very loud sounds like explosions may be heard 186 miles (300 km) away.

Sound waves travel through air at 1,125 feet (343 m) per second, or roughly 12.5 miles (20 km) per minute.

vocal cords

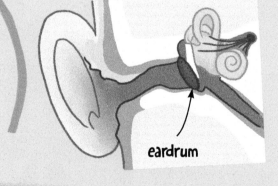

eardrum

Forensic scientists can use this knowledge—together with witness statements—to work out exactly where a sound came from.

Project: Fireworks Frenzy!

Someone set off really loud fireworks at around midnight last night, waking up everyone for a long distance in every direction. The first complaint calls came in to the police station at 12:01 a.m. from point A, 12:00 a.m. from point B, and 12:02 a.m. from point C. All the callers had called immediately after hearing the first firework. Armed with the knowledge that sound travels at roughly 12.5 miles (20 km) per minute, mark on the map where you think the fireworks were set off.

Shatters and Splatters

A window has been smashed. The pattern of broken glass can tell you whether the window was hit from the inside or the outside, and even by what tool. Forensic scientists also study how liquids such as paint or blood behave when splattered.

If a robber breaks a window, tiny pieces of glass, less than 0.04 inches (1 mm) across, can stick in their hair and clothing. This evidence proves they made the smash!

When a window is smashed, larger fragments of glass land close to the window, mostly in the direction of the blow.

Smaller fragments can travel up to 13 feet (4 m) in all directions.

Project: Splatter Patterns

Do this experiment outdoors to avoid spoiling anything with paint. Ask an adult to cut the tops off 6 raw eggs. Empty the shells, then wash and fill each with a different shade of paint. Draw up a chart to record 6 egg drops.

You will need:

- Old clothes and protective glasses
- 6 (or more) eggs
- Washable paints
- Extra-large sheets of paper
- Tape measure
- Notebook and pencil

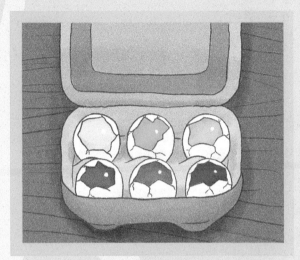

1. You need columns for "Height of Drop," "Width of Splatter," and "Other Findings."

2. Choose a height for your first egg drop. Record the exact height in your table.

3. Drop your first egg! Record the width of the splatter and its shape. Drop the other 5 eggs from different heights.

4. Increase the height of your drops by 1 foot (30.5 cm) each time. To drop an egg from high up, ask an adult to use a ladder.

When the eggs are dropped, they are pulled to the ground by gravity. Gravity makes objects go faster and faster as they fall.

You should notice that the splatters get larger when the eggs are dropped from a greater height. This is because they hit the ground with greater force.

Melting Mayhem

Heat melts many materials from a solid into a liquid. Ice melts into water at 32°F (0°C), styrofoam melts at 464°F (240°C), and gold at 1,948°F (1,064°C). Could this information solve crimes? Imagine that a fire at a warehouse has melted styrofoam cups but not gold plates. This means it burned between 464°F (240°C) and 1,948°F (1,064°C)—a clue about what started it.

It is hard to believe, but metals will also turn into gas if they get really really hot. Melted gold starts evaporating into gas at around 5,070°F (2,800°C).

Water can exist in three states—solid, liquid, and gas.

At 32°F (0°C), ice melts into liquid water.

At 212°F (100°C), water boils and starts to evaporate as a gas.

Project: Ice Pop Puzzle!

It is a hot, sunny day, and someone has snatched an ice pop without paying for it. Which dripping ice pop trail leads from the ice pop stall to the thief?

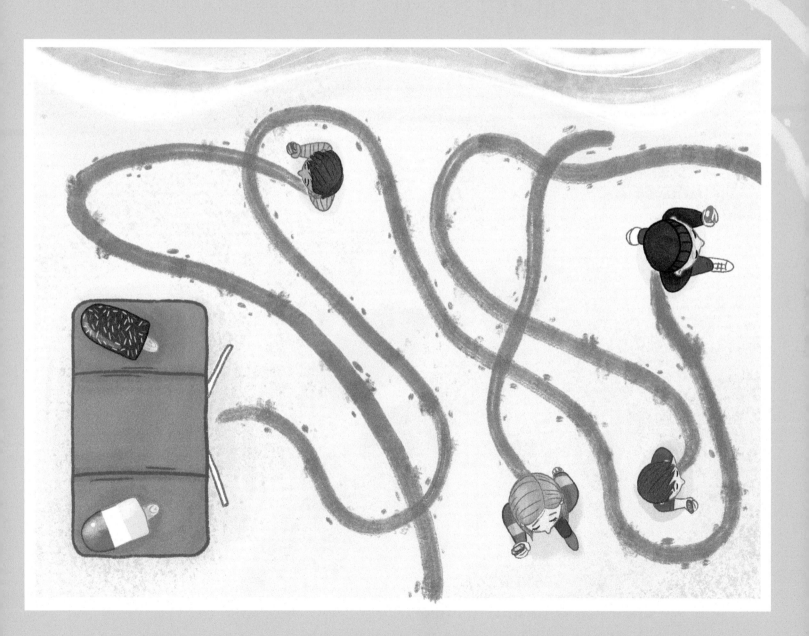

Watch for Reactions

A chemical reaction happens when two materials react to each other, causing a change to both materials. For example, you create a chemical reaction when you bake a cake. The materials—including eggs and flour—change when they are mixed together and heated in the oven.

To find invisible fingerprints, scientists use an iodine spray. Iodine reacts to the oil and sweat in fingerprints, turning them bright orange.

The chemical luminol glows when it reacts to the iron in blood, which can reveal a bloodstain even if someone has wiped it up.

Forensic scientists use chemical reactions to find substances that are invisible to the naked eye.

Project: Make Invisible Ink!

Making invisible ink is a lot of fun! You can pretend you are a secret agent as you keep all your secret codes and messages hidden from others. All you need are some basic household objects and the hidden power of lemon juice.

You will need:

- Half of a lemon
- Water
- Spoon
- Bowl
- Cotton swab
- White paper
- Hair dryer

1. Draw a simple map of your room, using pencils, wax crayons, or marker pens.

What's going on?
Lemon juice is an organic substance that oxidizes and turns brown when heated. Diluting the lemon juice in water makes it very hard to notice when you apply it to the paper—no one will be aware of its presence until it is heated and the secret message is revealed.

2. Dip the cotton swab in the lemon juice, and mark a big X where you've hidden some treasure (this can be a note for your friend or a little toy). Wait for it to dry.

3. Give the map to your friend—who won't be able to see the lemon juice mark! But gently heat the map with the hair dryer, and you'll see a brown X emerging ...

Identify the Powder

Forensic scientists often need to identify unknown substances. That white powder may be an explosive, a poison, a drug, or just flour. To find out, take it to the lab for testing. Never touch an unknown substance with bare hands, don't taste or sniff it, and wear safety clothing to do experiments.

To identify an unknown substance, a forensic scientist can use these methods:

1. Examine the substance—using a microscope if necessary—to see if it looks like any known substances.

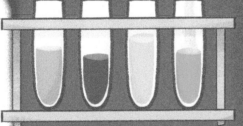

2. Find out if the substance chemically reacts (see page 30) to any other substances.

3. Note how the substance behaves when added to water—does it sink, float, or dissolve? Some powdery solids seem to disappear in water because they spread evenly through it. This is called dissolving.

Project: Design Your Own Experiment!

Exercise your science skills by designing your own experiment to tell apart flour, salt, and sugar. Of course, you know which is which already—but how are you going to prove it scientifically using only the listed equipment?

Your "Unknown" Substances:

- Flour
- Salt
- Sugar

You Can Use this Equipment:

- A drinking glass
- A tablespoon
- Tap water
- A clock or timer that can count in seconds
- Paper and pencil

Design a step-by-step experiment to identify the 3 substances. Consider how to measure out quantities, take timings, and record your observations.

Hint: These substances behave differently when they are added to water. One of them does not dissolve in water—it will make the water cloudy, then settle on the bottom of the glass. The other two substances dissolve in water, but one dissolves more quickly than the other.

Sugar

Flour

Find the Fabric

If you are lucky, a robber will have left behind fluff from a sweater, a scrap of torn jacket on a broken window, or a snag from a sock on a fence. Forensic scientists can identify the fabric and whether it matches a suspect's sweater, jacket, or socks. They come to their conclusions based on the fabric's dye, construction, and properties.

Fabric can have a range of different properties. Properties can be seen, felt, or measured.

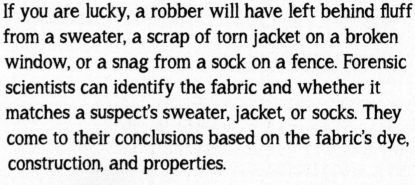

Transparent fabrics are see-through. Opaque fabrics cannot be seen through.

Waterproof fabrics do not let water pass through them. Absorbent fabrics soak up water easily.

Strong fabrics are hard to tear. Weak fabrics are easy to rip.

Elastic fabrics can be stretched. Rigid fabrics are hard to bend.

Project: Identify the Scrap!

While you are investigating a break-in at the swimming pool, you notice a piece of yellow fabric caught on the broken wood of the door. You take the fabric back to the laboratory for analysis. Based on the properties of the fabric, which item do you think it came from?

Properties of the Scrap:

- Opaque
- Waterproof
- Strong
- Not elastic
- Not rigid

Possible Sources of the Fabric:

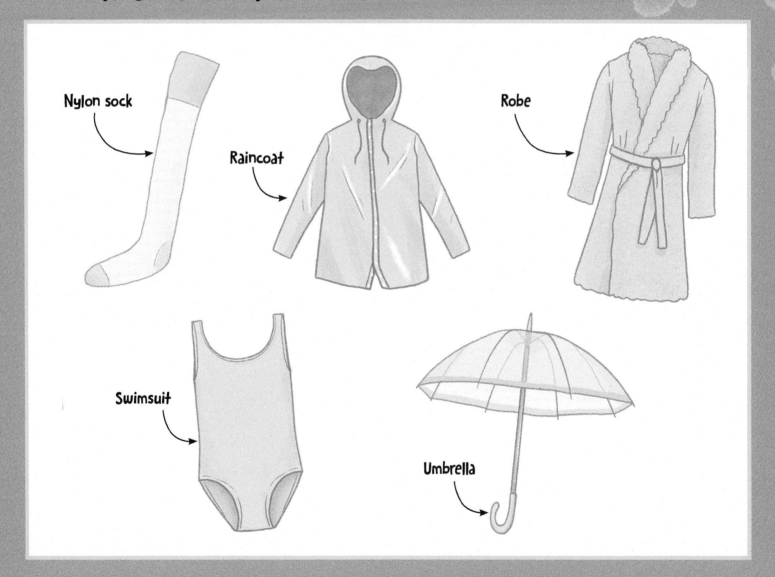

Nylon sock

Raincoat

Robe

Swimsuit

Umbrella

Magnetic Attraction

Everything on Earth is made of building blocks called atoms. Inside atoms are electrons that spin. Electrons spinning in one direction create an invisible force called magnetism. This happens in a small number of metals, including iron, nickel, and cobalt. These metals are attracted to magnets and can also become magnets.

A magnetic field surrounds the poles. Magnetic metals within this invisible field will be attracted or repelled.

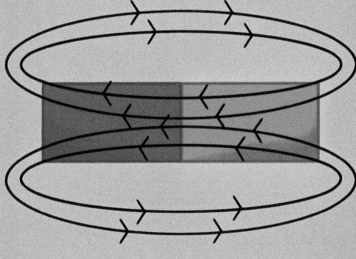

Magnets have a north pole and a south pole. The north pole of one magnet attracts the south pole and repels the north pole of another magnet.

Forensic scientists use magnetism to find buried metal objects, from coins to weapons.

Project: Magnet Attack!

A thief is terrorizing antique shops around the world, using a hidden magnet to steal priceless objects. Which of these objects is at risk of being stolen from Miss Ming's Antique Shop?

China vase

Copper bracelet

Nickel coin

Diamond pendant

Cobalt ring

Gold pin

Copper necklace

Glass bottle

Iron brooch

Silver earrings

Magic Microorganisms

Microorganisms are life forms like bacteria and fungi. These settle on dead animals and plants. As they feed, they grow in number. The amount of growth will tell a forensic scientist how long a substance has been lying around.

These microorganisms do a vital job. As they feed, they help to break down dead plants, animals, and waste. If nothing decayed, the planet would be piled high with garbage!

Bacteria exist in three main shapes—spirals, rods, and spheres. Thousands of bacteria could fit on the dot at the end of this sentence.

Fungi range from tiny microorganisms to large mushrooms and toadstools.

Project: Grow Fungi!

To study the growth of microorganisms, try this experiment to grow fungi on bread. Fungi spores are like the seeds of a fungus. Spores are all around us, so they will land on the bread without your help.

You will need:

- 3 slices of bread
- A bowl of water
- 3 zip-seal freezer bags
- Paper and pencil

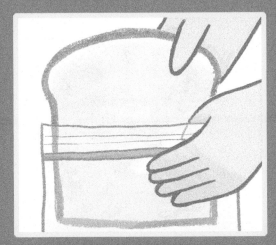

1. Dunk each slice of bread in the water. Put each slice in its own zip-seal freezer bag, then seal the bag tightly.

2. Put the first bag in the freezer; the second in a warm spot, such as by a radiator; and the third at "room temperature."

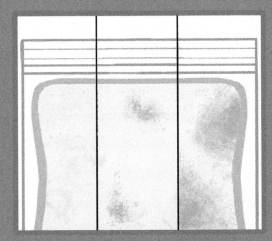

3. Without opening the bags, check on the growth of microorganisms on the bread after 5, 7, and 10 days. Write down your observations, as well as predictions about future growth.

4. Throw away the bags without opening them!

Once you have sealed the bags, do not reopen them, because you will release fungi spores into the air. This could make you sick, particularly if you have allergies.

Spreading Infection

Some microorganisms cause illness in humans. Viruses cause infectious diseases that pass from person to person, such as chicken pox. Some bacteria cause illnesses such as stomach upsets from eating dirty food. Many forensic scientists are experts on disease-causing microorganisms and can tell when an outbreak began.

More than 200 different viruses cause colds.

Cold viruses travel from an infected person in coughs and sneezes or in snot wiped onto objects.

For 1 to 3 days, the "incubation period," the infected person has no symptoms, although the virus has invaded the cells in their nose, mouth, and throat.

The infected person's body fights back. Symptoms appear—sore throat, runny nose, coughing, headache, and fever—and may last 7-10 days.

Project: Who Spread the Infection?

A burglar broke into the Infectious Disease Laboratory, breaking a vial containing the Green Spot virus and becoming infected immediately. Seven days after the break-in, three suspects have arrived at the police station for questioning. Which suspect could have committed the burglary?

Facts about the Green Spot virus:

- Incubation period is 3 days.
- The only symptom is large green spots.
- Spots last 5 days.
- The sufferer is highly infectious as soon as the spots appear.

The Suspects:

Suspect A
Seven days after the break-in, Suspect A has no spots, and neither do her family and friends.

Suspect B
Seven days after the break-in, Suspect B has green spots, but his family and friends do not.

Suspect C
Seven days after the break-in, Suspect C has green spots and so do her family and friends.

Analyzing Handwriting

Strange as it seems, some criminals may write a letter to a newspaper or the police. Handwriting experts try to match the handwriting to samples of writing from suspects. Experts might also be called in when someone is suspected of forging someone else's signature on a document.

Look at loops and curls on g, y, f, and j.

Are all the letters connected to each other or separate?

The quick brown fox jumps over the lazy dog.
The quick brown fox jumps over the lazy dog.
The quick brown fox jumps over the lazy dog.
The quick brown fox jumps over the lazy dog.
The quick brown fox jumps over the lazy dog.

Are upstrokes vertical or slanted?

Handwriting experts look at these key points:

1. The ways the letters are formed—everyone writes each letter a little differently.

2. The style of writing—the way handwriting is taught has changed over the years and differs from region to region.

3. The smoothness and darkness of the lines show how hard the writer presses and how fast they write.

4. Signs that the writer is disguising their handwriting. Shaky starts and lots of pen lifts reveal they are writing slowly and possibly copying.

Project: Match the Handwriting!

A bicycle thief left a rude note for the bike's owner. Handwriting samples have been supplied by three suspects. Who wrote the note?

Note Left at the Crime Scene:

I stole yOUr bike! Ha ha!

Handwriting Samples from Suspects:

Suspect A — I stole your bike!

Suspect B — I stole your bike!

Suspect C — I stole your bike!

No two samples of handwriting from one person will be completely identical! Look for similarities between samples, but also watch out for differences that could rule out any suspects.

Ink Test

Another way to find out who wrote a note is to match its ink with the ink in a suspect's pen. The method for doing this is called chromatography. Ink is a mixture of different pigments, or shades. Chromatography separates the pigments so we can see them. The method can also match the dye in a scrap of cloth with the dye in a suspect's clothing.

Banks may protect their money with packets of dye, which are exploded by remote control if the money is stolen. Chromatography matches the dye on a suspect's hands and face with the bank's dye.

Even black inks are mixtures of different pigments.

Project: Separate the Inks!

Try your hand at chromatography yourself. When the water is absorbed by the paper towel, the pigments dissolve in the water. Some molecules of pigments are smaller and lighter than others, so they travel farther up the paper. That is why the pigments separate. Try to predict which pigments each ink will split into.

You will need:

- Paper towel
- Water
- 4 drinking glasses
- Washable marker pens in black, red, blue, and green

1. Cut the paper towel into 4 strips about 2 inches (5 cm) wide and around 10 inches (25 cm) long. Pour about 1/4 inch (0.5 cm) of water into each glass.

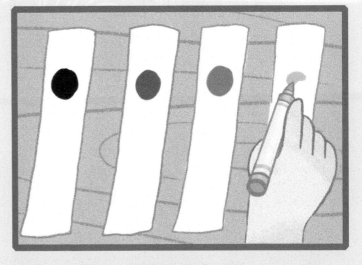

2. On each strip of paper towel, make a large spot with a different marker pen, about 1 inch (2.5 cm) from the bottom.

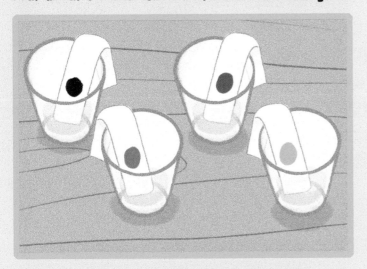

3. Place the spotted end of each strip in a glass, making sure the spot does not go in the water. Fold over the top of the towel to keep it from slipping.

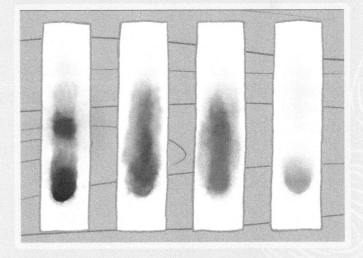

4. Watch as the water is absorbed by the towel, splitting the ink as it travels up the paper. Let the strips dry, and then examine the pigments.

Computer Crime

The police can solve crimes from information on computers and phones, such as emails, text messages, and files—even deleted files. The time of a text message or email could prove where a suspect was. The content of a message could prove that a criminal mastermind gave the order to rob a bank!

The letters at the end of a computer file's name are called "filename extensions." They give clues about what sort of file it is:

Files names that end in .mp3 contain sounds, such as songs.

File names that end in .jpeg are usually photos.

File names that end in .doc or .docx contain mostly words.

Did you know that whenever you look at a website, you leave a record on your computer or phone? So don't look at a website called www.getawaydrivers.com if you are planning to rob a bank!

File names that end in .xls contain tables and charts.

Project: File Forensics!

A bank has been robbed, and a suspect has been arrested for the crime. Examine the list of files found on their computer. Find 3 files that may contain evidence.

List of Files:

- birthdayparty.jpeg
- cutedog.jpeg
- happybirthday.mp3
- fluffykitten.jpeg
- funnykitten.jpeg
- hairydog.jpeg

- howtocrackasafe.doc
- jinglebells.mp3
- lonesomeblues.mp3
- mewithfriend.jpeg
- naughtykitten.jpeg

- newyorkbank.jpeg
- prettyflower.jpeg
- robberyschedule.xls
- christmaslist.doc
- seaside.jpeg
- wewishyouamerrychristmas.mp3

Phone Finder

When you make a call on your smartphone, it sends your words through the air as radio waves. These are picked up by a nearby phone tower, which can send and receive radio waves over large distances. A network of towers sends your radio waves to the phone of the person you are talking with.

Information from phone towers can reveal not just where someone made a call but also whether they were on the move.

Even when you are not making a call, your phone sends out radio waves. These contain your phone number, so if a phone is switched on, it can be traced to within about 160 feet (50 m).

The caller was in one spot for the whole call.

The caller moved past several phone towers while they talked.

Project: Find the Injured Hiker!

A hiker has called Mountain Rescue to say that he has twisted his ankle somewhere along a remote mountain track. Using information from the local phone towers, we have discovered that his phone is 5 miles (8 km) from phone tower A and 10 miles (16 km) from phone tower B. Use this map of the track and a ruler to find out where the injured hiker is.

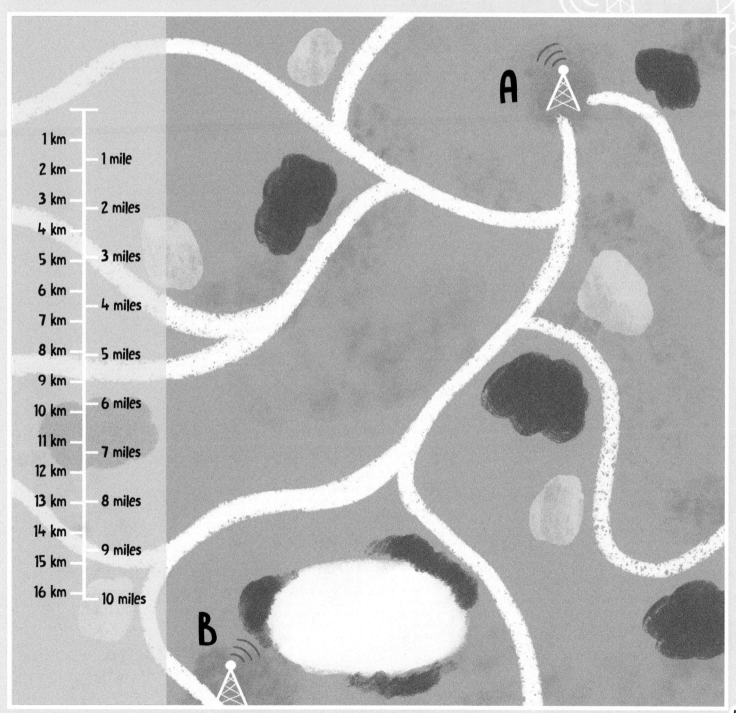

A Worthy Witness?

When there are witnesses to a crime, it is important to make a careful note of their memories. Try to judge what is true or not, and what is important and what is not. Witnesses can forget details, get confused, or be influenced by others.

If you remembered everything that ever happened, your brain would overload! Your brain selects what you need to remember and how long to remember it for.

Some memories are not needed for long (like remembering to put your snack in your bag). The brain stores these for a short time, then forgets them!

Some things seem unimportant (like the number of windows in the house you just walked past), so they are not remembered at all.

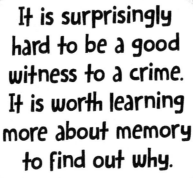

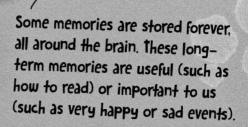

It is surprisingly hard to be a good witness to a crime. It is worth learning more about memory to find out why.

Some memories are stored forever, all around the brain. These long-term memories are useful (such as how to read) or important to us (such as very happy or sad events).

Project: Witness Statement!

How good a witness do you think you would be? How strong do you think your long-term and short-term memories are? Try this exercise to find out more.

Write down what you did yesterday for each hour of the day.

Now write down what you did four weeks ago on Saturday.

What have you learned about your memory? Were some things easier to remember than others? Did you have to make guesses?

Assessing Alibis

An alibi is a claim that a suspect was in a different place when a crime was committed, proving that they could not have done it. An excellent alibi would be giving a speech in front of an audience at exactly the time a crime took place! Most alibis need to be investigated.

You may need to do calculations to check alibis. For example:
A suspect owns a car with a maximum speed of 50 mph (80 km/h). They were definitely in Smalltown at 9 a.m. A crime took place 100 miles (160 km) away in Bigtown at 10 a.m. Could the suspect have reached Bigtown in time to commit the crime? The answer is no! Driving at 50 mph (80 km/h), it would have taken the suspect 2 hours to travel 100 miles (160 km), reaching Bigtown no earlier than 11 a.m.

Look for other people to corroborate, or back up, a suspect's alibi. Hunt for evidence, such as movie tickets or images from security cameras, that proves a suspect was where he or she claims to have been.

Project: Check that Alibi!

Someone stole all the bananas from the supermarket in Bluetown at 4 p.m. yesterday afternoon. Read these statements given by three possible suspects, then figure out who does not have an alibi.

Suspect A

Yesterday afternoon, I walked my dog Charlie in Bluetown Park. There, I bumped into my friend Beth, who was walking her dog Pepper, at around 3 p.m. Then I drove to Main Street in Redtown to watch a movie, which finished at 5:30 p.m. I dropped off Charlie at my friend Carla's house just before the movie started. Luckily, Carla lives right on Main Street.

Suspect B

Yesterday evening, I was playing Dorothy in Bluetown's performance of *The Wizard of Oz*. The show started at 7 p.m. I went to the supermarket at around 3:45 p.m. to pick up cookies for the cast before our rehearsal, which began at 4:15 p.m. After picking up the cookies, I drove to Fiona's Flowers over in Yellowtown, about 12 miles (20 km) away, to buy flowers for our director, Viv.

Suspect C

Yesterday afternoon, I walked my poodle Pepper in Bluetown Park. I bumped into my friend Emma there, who was walking her dog Charlie. After saying goodbye to Emma, I drank some lemonade in the park café. I probably stayed in the café for about 30 minutes, chatting with the café owner. A bit later, I went to see a performance of *The Wizard of Oz*, which my friend Viv directed.

Detecting Lies

In some countries, including the United States, "lie detector" machines are used to try to tell if a suspect is lying. They test for signs of nervousness, such as a fast heartbeat. Unfortunately, innocent people can get nervous, and guilty people who are used to telling lies can pass them!

When we feel nervous or afraid, the brain releases hormones that give us a burst of energy, so we can run away from or fight the danger. Here are some signs that those hormones have been released:

Never believe that a suspect is guilty until you have collected and tested evidence—and, most importantly, before they have received a trial in a court of law.

1. Faster heartbeat.

2. Faster breathing.

3. Quicker blinking.

4. Blushing and sweating.

5. Pursed lips because of a dry mouth.

Project: Take Your Pulse!

Your heart is a muscle that pumps blood around your body by squeezing. Every time the heart squeezes, it sends a wave, or pulse, of blood through your veins. You can feel this pulse most easily where a vein passes over a bone, such as at your wrist. Try this experiment to see the effect of exercise on your pulse.

You will need:

- A stopwatch
- Paper and pencil
- A partner

1. To find the pulse on your wrist, place two fingers at the base of your thumb, then slide your fingers straight down onto your wrist. Press gently until you feel a faint, throbbing pulse.

2. Ask your partner to start the stopwatch. Count how many times you feel your pulse in 1 minute. Your partner should say "Stop" when the minute is up.

3. Now run on the spot for 1 minute.

4. As soon as you stop running, ask your partner to start the stopwatch. Count how many times you feel your pulse in 1 minute.

5. Compare the two heart rates. What do you notice?

Get to Work!

Forensic science is always improving. In ancient times, science was hardly ever used to solve crimes because people knew little about the human body, materials, or forces. Slowly, and particularly in the last 150 years, scientists have developed new tests and tools to solve crimes.

Did you know these forensic science records?

If you would like to be a forensic scientist, pay attention in science class at school, train yourself to notice details and to take careful notes, and always be honest and fair.

In 1888, photographs were first used to record the details of crime scenes.

The first crime was solved using fingerprint evidence in 1892.

In 1910, the first police laboratory was set up for examining trace evidence.

In 1984, the first police department was set up to solve crimes using computer evidence.

DNA evidence was first used to solve crimes in the 1980s.

Project: First Steps!

Now that you are a forensic scientist, you have arrived at your first crime scene. You should take the following steps, but in what order?

A Put evidence in clean bags or boxes, then seal and label them. Write your name on the seals so no one can open the evidence without you noticing.

B Without disturbing anything, survey the crime scene. Decide what types of evidence may be present and how to collect them.

C Search for trace and DNA evidence.

D Photograph the scene, making sure your photos show the location of every piece of evidence you have found. Make careful notes about all the details.

E Put on clean gloves, mask, and suit. Seal off the crime scene with police tape, so that no one can enter without permission.

F Make sure that the sealed evidence is taken to the police laboratory by yourself or a trusted officer. Keep a record of every bag and box.

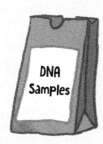

DNA Samples

Hair Samples

G Ask the police officer who has taken charge of the crime scene for information.

Pop Quiz

Have you been paying attention? Try answering these questions to test all of your newly acquired forensic knowledge.

1. Is this a loop or a whorl fingerprint pattern?

2. True or false? Your DNA is the same as your mother's, and different from your cousin.

3. List three different types of trace evidence that you might look for at a crime scene.

4. Why do forensic scientists wear masks, gloves, protective suits, and shoe covers? Is it:
    A) So that police officers can easily identify forensic scientists.
    B) So that they don't get their own clothes dirty.
    C) Because it's important that the scientists don't contaminate the scene with anything from their own bodies, clothes, or shoes.

5. How fast do sound waves travel through the air?
    A) 111 ft/second (34 m/second)
    B) 1,125 ft/second (343 m/second)
    C) 2 miles/second (3,434 m/second)

6. Try to guess from the filename alone which of these is likely to be a song, which is likely to be a picture, and which is likely to be a text file:
    shopping.doc
    holidays.jpg
    mynumberone.mp3

7. Which 5 of these signs <u>might</u> indicate that a suspect is telling a lie?

faster heartbeat
eye-rolling
dribbling
pursed lips
slower blinking
faster breathing
sneezing
blushing or sweating
faster blinking
hiccups

8. True or false: Witnesses always agree on the facts—if there are differences in their accounts, it means that one of them is lying.

9. How many teeth does an adult human usually have?
A) 32
B) 36
C) 40

10. If you found a pen that you thought a suspect had used, what might you look for to confirm your suspicions—fingerprints or DNA?

Write down your answers here, and check them on page 61.

1 ....

2 ....

3 ....

4 ....

5 ....

6 ....

7 ....

8 ....

9 ....

10 ....

Answers

P. 5 Bag 3 contains all the necessary items.

P. 9 Suspect 4: Percy the Pig ate all the cookies.

P. 11

P. 15 It may be worth calling in Suspect C for questioning.

P. 17

P. 19 Suspect 3 bit into the chocolate.

P. 23 Suspect 3 could have cast the shadow.

P. 25 The fireworks were set off somewhere near point B.

P. 29

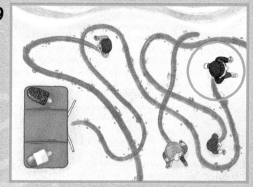

P. 33 Drop one tablespoon of each substance into a fresh glass of water. Start a timer when the substance enters the water. Stir continuously to try to dissolve the substance. The tablespoon of flour will not dissolve. When you stop stirring, it will sink to the bottom of the glass. The tablespoon of sugar will dissolve faster than the salt. The greater the quantity of sugar and salt, the longer they will take to dissolve and the greater the time difference between them.

P. 35 The fabric was ripped from the raincoat.

P. 37 The iron brooch, nickel coin, and cobalt ring are made from magnetic metals and are at risk of being stolen.

p. 41 Based on the symptoms of Suspect C and her family and friends, she could have carried out the break-in.

p. 43 Suspect B wrote the note.

p. 47 The files howtocrackasafe.doc, newyorkbank.jpeg, and robberyschedule.xls may be worth examining.

p. 49

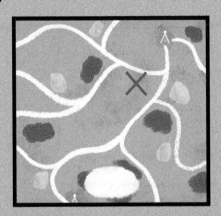

p. 53 Suspect A was probably dropping off her dog at Carla's house in Redtown at 4 p.m. Check with Carla that this alibi is true. Suspect B was probably buying flowers in Yellowtown at 4 p.m. Check with Fiona's Flowers to make sure. Suspect C has no alibi for 4 p.m. Suspect C met Suspect A and her dog Charlie in Bluetown Park at around 3 p.m., then spent half an hour in the park café. We do not know where she was between 3.30 p.m. and 7 p.m., when the performance of *The Wizard of Oz* began.

p. 57 The correct order of steps is: G E B C D A F.

pp. 58–59

1. It is a whorl fingerprint pattern.

2. False. You get half of your DNA from your biological mother and half from your biological father, so no other person in the world has exactly the same DNA as you (unless you're an identical twin!).

3. You might look for some of the following:
   - footprints
   - fingerprints
   - body fluids
   - hair
   - soil/dirt
   - paint
   - broken glass
   - tiny pieces of clothes.

4. C.

5. B.

6. shopping.doc is likely to be a text file. holidays.jpg is likely to be a picture. mynumberone.mp3 is likely to be a song.

7. faster heartbeat
   pursed lips
   faster breathing
   blushing or sweating
   faster blinking

8. False. People often remember things slightly differently, so differences don't necessarily mean that someone is deliberately lying.

9. A.

10. Both! You might also want to compare the ink on the note to the ink in the pen to see if they match.

Glossary

Alibi Evidence showing that a person was somewhere else when a crime was committed.

Analysis Careful examination of something in order to understand it.

Bacteria Microorganisms with just one cell; some can cause illness in humans.

Body fluids Liquids made in the human body, such as blood and tears.

Cell A tiny building block from which living things are made. All living things are either single cells or are made from many cells working together.

Chemical reaction A change that takes place when two or more substances combine to form a new substance.

Chromatography A method of separating a mixture into its different parts.

Corroborate To confirm or support something, such as an idea or statement.

Decay To rot or decompose through the action of bacteria and fungi.

Decode Convert a coded message into an understandable one.

Density The weight of an object compared to the amount of space it fills.

Diameter The distance of a straight line from side to side passing through the midpoint of a circle.

Dissolve When a solid is mixed into a liquid and becomes part of it.

DNA (deoxyribonucleic acid) The material found in the cells of nearly all living things that controls the growth and work of cells. The instructions contained in DNA are passed down from parents to their children.

Eardrum A thin skin within each ear that moves backward and forward very quickly when reached by sound waves.

Evaporate To change from a liquid into a gas.

Evidence Information or materials that prove whether or not something is true. Evidence can be used in a court of law to try to prove the facts about a crime.

Eyewitnesses People who saw a crime happen.

Forensic scientists Experts who use scientific methods to collect and test evidence in order to solve crimes. Science is the study of natural things through careful observation and experimentation.

Forging Making a copy of something in order to deceive, or trick.

Fungi Living things that get their food from rotting material or other living things.

Gravity A force that pulls all objects toward each other. The larger the object, the greater the pull of its gravity, so Earth's gravity is much greater than a child's.

Incubation period The time between being exposed to an infection and getting the first symptoms.

Iodine A purplish chemical that is found naturally on Earth.

Laboratory A room or building set up for scientific experiments and research.

Liquid A substance that flows, such as water, milk, or vinegar.

Luminol A man-made chemical that can be made to glow bright blue through chemical reactions.

Microorganisms Living things too small to be seen without the help of a microscope.

Microscope An instrument that uses lenses to view very small objects and living things.

Molecule A group of atoms that are joined to each other.

Nucleus The "brain" of a cell that helps control its function, including growth and reproduction. It contains a person's hereditary information from their parents.

Opaque Not able to be seen through.

Pigment A substance that gives black, white, or another color to materials.

Pollen A powder made by the male parts of a flower. When the female parts of a flower receive pollen, they can produce seeds.

Properties The qualities of matter that can be seen, felt, or measured.

Radio waves Invisible energy that can travel through the air. Radio waves are often used for sending communications, such as radio and television shows or phone conversations.

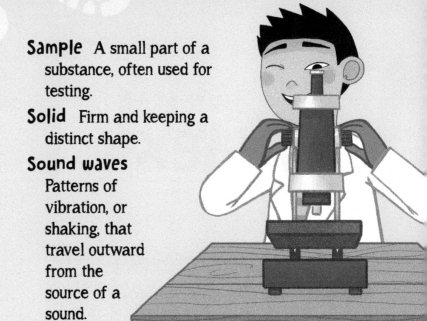

Sample A small part of a substance, often used for testing.

Solid Firm and keeping a distinct shape.

Sound waves Patterns of vibration, or shaking, that travel outward from the source of a sound.

Spores Cells produced by fungi, bacteria, and some other living things that can grow into new fungi or bacteria.

Suspect A person thought possibly to be guilty of a crime.

Symptoms Changes in the body and brain caused by a disease.

Trace evidence Materials left behind while committing a crime, including hair, scraps or threads of clothing, soil, and glass.

Translucent Able to be seen through, but objects on the other side look unclear.

Transparent Able to be seen through, so that objects on the other side are clear.

Unique Unlike anything else.

Vibrate To move quickly to and fro.

Viruses Microorganisms that can only reproduce (make copies of themselves) inside the cells of other living things. Viruses can cause illness.

Index

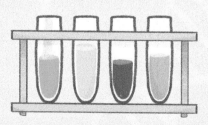